I0390678

Faye Love

Poems

By
Sky Boivin

Other Books By Sky Boivin
Poetry:
An Assortment of Poetry
Scattered Emotions
Inspired Thoughts
Random Thoughts
Something Loved
Anger Withheld
A Twisted Vine
The Alice Poems
Faye Love
Collection of Poetry

Other books:
Life Without You
Their Hope Within The Flames
GrayScaleGods QueenFaye Solos

Special thanks to those who inspired these poems. My role play partner, for retweeting some tweets and in our daily writings. The retweeted accounts that were shared and a few in passing messages when I needed that last few poems. Many thanks in the help. Keep inspiring and being inspired.

ALWAYS AND FOREVER

You breathe life back into me.
All this time,
Lost in darkness.
Light and love, unknown to me.
Shines now from your eyes,
Resonates into me.
I've once thought I had become nothing.
Becoming frozen,
Until you.
Now, I can't imagine life without.
Always and forever shall it always be.
Love to be held long and true.
Endless kisses, Endless caresses.
Nights, hoping that never end.
Like in a dream,
You are still there come morning.
Reaffirming,
Always and forever holds strong still.
Kind hearted and caring.
Endless whispers never to end.
Always and forever,
Shall our love remain.

6.19.2018

A New Hope

New found hope
For the last few years,
It was sad tears upon my pillow at night.
Starting with loss,
And then just loneliness and pain.
Such overwhelming sadness engulfed me.
I dared not know how to swim out.
Slowly I climbed up
Yet, the tears remained to stain my pillow
Then you came along.
As the days grew past,
More and more we became.
Only smiles upon my pillow.
No more sad tears.
Just happiness of being needed,
Wanted as I am.
Not in a golden cage of unrelenting
demands and ideals that can never be to pass.
Allowed to be as I am,
Nothing but kindness and love,
From such a wonderful soul
Now fills my soul with new found hope
And smiles.
I've found peace.

8.27.2018

The twins

after months of waiting.
Anticipation growing each day.
Our little girls.
Tiny toes, Tiny noses.
Little fingers wrapping around
His one finger.
Staring at such wonder and awe.
Your tiny empresses.
Filling your heart with such
Overwhelming love
At the sight.

Watching from across the room
Silently smiling.
Tiny noses, tiny mouths.
Tiny versions of us.
Two becomes four in an instant.
Family, love
Always and forever
Coming to my mind.

12.5.2018

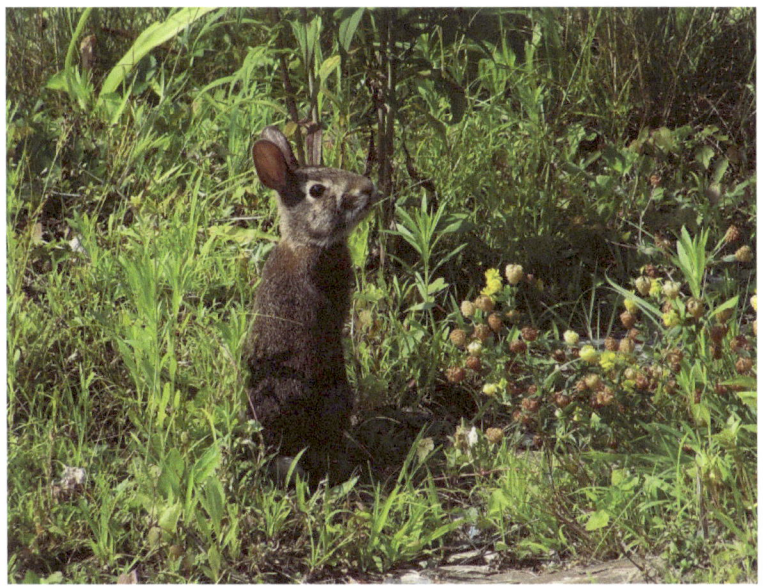

Our Story

first glances, first words,
One night, by a piano.
Nights pass, sharing songs
Sharing poetry
Smiles, laughter, and music.
Before we knew it,
First kisses, caresses.
Long nights shared.
A proposal
    Wedding bliss
All seems a dream.
And this, beautiful this.

A family
Never promised to be for you.
Always dreamed,
But never allowed to be.
Now a reality.
Now a promised sun on the horizon,
Just within grasp.
Moonlight glows
Dragon eggs bound
And many other adventures
To come our way
For such a blessing
These girls shall be

11.16.2018

Los Amantes del Tiempo (the lovers of time)

Mi encanto, he whispers in the dark
She smiles to feather light kisses along her skin.
She whispers back, mí corazón,
The dark is just as beautiful.
he agrees to the sound of the phrase,
Continuing to kiss her under her ear.
She returns as she is lost to his touch,
For the darkest nights have the brightest stars.
As he caresses her waist,
They delay their kisses as the night unfolds around them.
They notice nothing as their love blossoms more.
For they are los amantes del tiempo.
They are lovers of time,
Because time means nothing to a vampire and a faye
Lost only to themselves in the evenings
And in the daylight hours
As their love grows more each day for each other.
Continued caresses of tresses and soft whispers
As they hold each other close to each other each night.
Guarding her dreams as she sleeps
As she is guarding his heart as he sleeps.
Los amantes del tiempo
Siempre y para siempre.

jan.5,2019

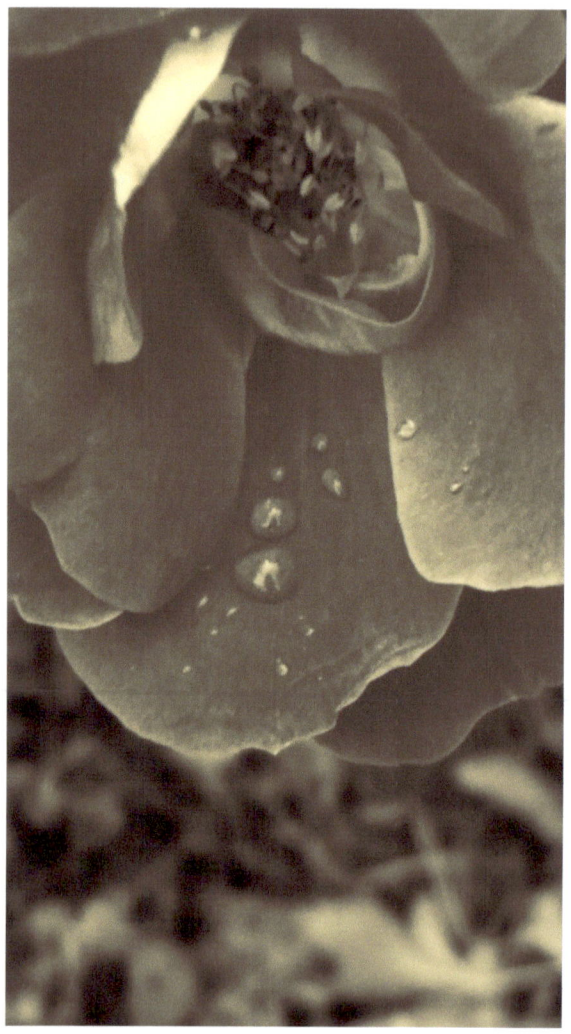

<u>checkmate</u>

She allowed me
To capture her Queen
I took her knowing
Checkmate was hers
It did not matter
She was Alice
And she was mine
She allowed it so
Forever I shall be hers

1.7.2019

Her magic

He calls her magic
Like any other force,
That compels him
But he does not fully understand.
So let's feed the fire slowly;
bank the embers
and allow the slow burn
to transport us beyond time.
It was just a kiss
between souls
and yet, he can't resist
the raw truth of a gentle heart.
Her miracles are simple;
Just physics, art and magic
As she whispers in the darkness
"You can't miss me
I'm there with you, always"

-1.10.2019

Such Mystery

The mystery
Isn't that we are together
Is how we could ever
Have been apart

All these months with each other
Endless night skies
Waking to beautiful sunrises
In each other's arms

Such mystery life can be in its ways
Of casualties and causalities
Not always together
Not always connected to the other

But not always apart
All at the same time
Interesting the way the fates
Can play in their games

Bringing two unknowing souls
Together in life
At just the precise moment
Of time when least expected

Ours was by piano and candlelight
Over songs and poetry
Such mystery
We have ever been apart

3.3.2019

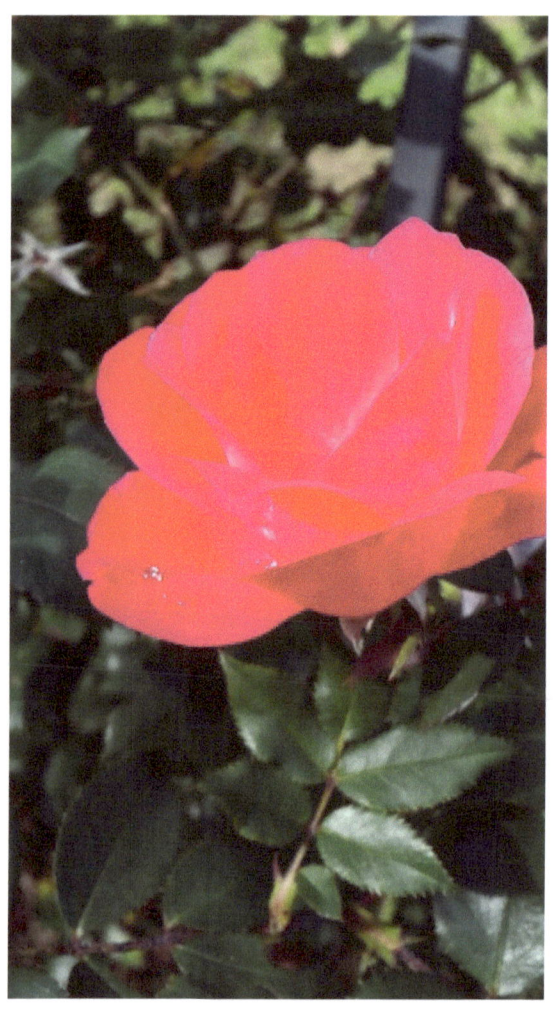

Dearest Sister

'I met her on day one
of the rest of forever'
he wrote home
to his dear beloved sister,
telling her all about
a love he found in a soul.
'a special soul
unlike any other'
he continued.
'she is the light
in my darkness
the reason
the dawn always comes'
the words flow
just like his music
on the piano keys
as he pours out
all he feels for his Faye.
'she is my unread book
My unfinished composition
She has become my life.'
He ends the letter
Seals it inside
To send it on its way.

3.10.2019

His Unfinished Manuscript

it was crazy to think
that it hasn't been that long
and yet,
it feels like an eternity.
A dream,
Made just for them.
She was his unread book.
So much more of her
He had yet to explore.
Hidden treasures
In locked rooms
Within her soul
Buried deep down
Within her.
She was his unfinished poem
His need to learn more
About her
Was a call so strong
It demanded to be complete.
She was his unfinished
Musical manuscript.
And he loved every note
That came from within her soul.

3.10.2019

Eternity

The stars and the universe
Were all one
Before time began
Just as you and I
Shall be so when it ends
But let us not dwell
On such thoughts
For now we have today
This moment of time
Forever in our grasp
Our time feels
Evermore as a dream
We can be lost away in
Away from the world
Which surrounds us
Lost in what we are
Lost in what we have
The stars and the universe
Were all one
Before time began
And we, my darling
Have eternity to share.

3.10.2019

Never Forget

please never forget
you wrote words
that so moved me
he whispers
in the darkness
hoping she hears him
where ever she has gone
I will never forget
He hears a faint sound
Upon the gentle breeze
Flowing through
The balcony doors
He suddenly feels
At ease sensing her words
He closes his eyes
Thinking on memories
Of feeling her there
In his arms
He opens his eyes
Sensing someone
And sees her before him
Never forget
They whisper to each other
As they embrace

3.10.2019

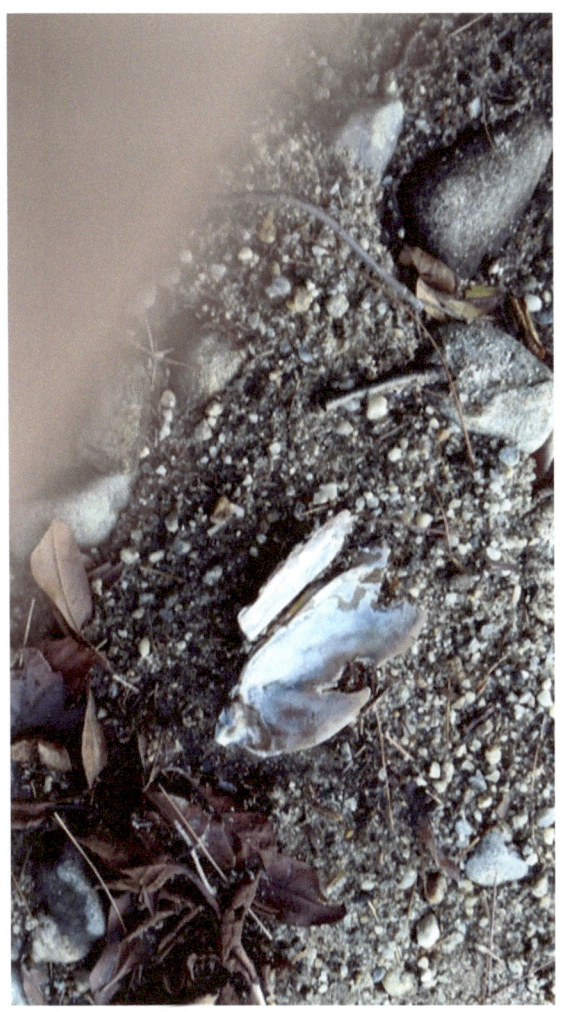

Always

I care
irrevocably and forever
nothing
will ever change that
I love
With all of my every being
Never
Will that be changed
I dream
Of endless nights
Hopeful
Of always and forever

3.10.2019

The Secret

the secret is
you are my music
my heart doesn't beat
without you
the secret is
you are my song
my soul ebbs and flows
just for you
the secret is
you are my poetry
my veins pulse
at the thoughts of you
the secret is
I love you

3.10.2019

Did He Know

Did he know
That he was her sunrise
On the first day of now,
Painting the clouds
All the colors of love.
Did he know
That he was her sunset
On the first day of forever,
Illuminating the world
just for them.
did he know
that he was her moonlight eve
making their path
glow with their love
did he know

3.10.2019

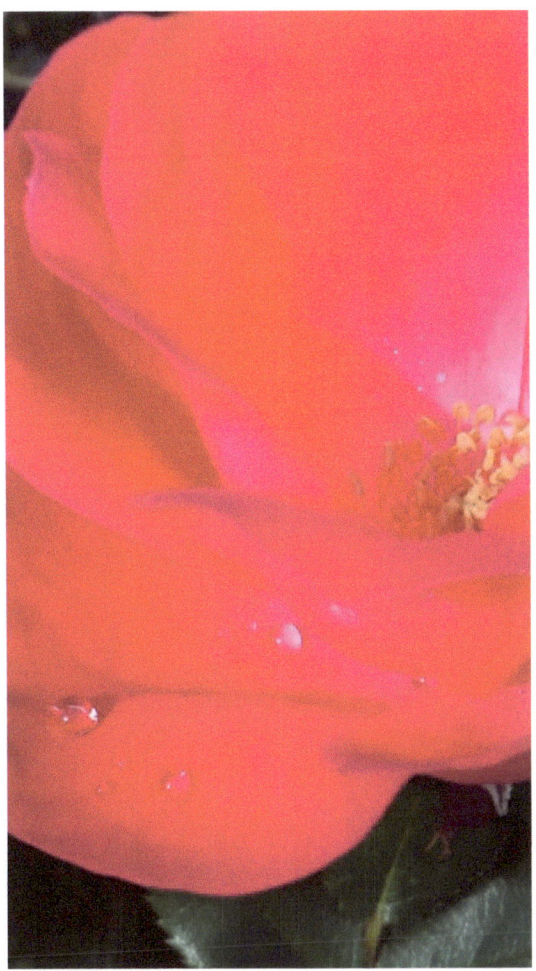

The Fire

She lights in his heart
A fire that never ends
She writes in places
His heart
Has forever longed
To be in
'I just thought I'd let you know
I happened to think of you
In this moment
And every moment before
You are the fire in my blood
The passion in every dream'
He writes lovingly
To his beloved charm
Then leaves it beside her
On their bed
With a single red rose
Set on top of it
For her to find when she wakes
Knowing the smile
That he will leave across her face

3.10.2019

By My Silence

As the soft patter of
The falling snow upon
The window outside,
She reaches out
Absently to reach for him.
Only to hold his pillow.
Her beloved heart has yet
To return home to her.
Unable now to drift back to sleep,
She slips on her headphones
She turns on their songs
In an attempt to drift back
As though the piano sounds
Will lull her to thinking
That he is really just
In the next room
Playing like he used to
To guard her dreams
Like he always does.
Only now, she misses his arms,
His warmth. His heart.
Just the thought of knowing
He was home safe with her.
Her beloved rey
Guarding her dreams
As she guards his heart.
Alas she will try to do so
From where they each are.
She shall try to dream
Of safe return and keep
him safe that way.
She listens to the soft patter
Of the snow as it falls outside

www.ingramcontent.com/pod-product-compliance
Lightning Source LLC
Chambersburg PA
CBHW041212180526
45172CB00006B/1247